WHAT MAKES A BRUEGEL A BRUEGEL?

Richard Mühlberger

The Metropolitan Museum of Art
Viking
NEW YORK

VIKING
First published in 1993 by The Metropolitan Museum of Art, New York, and Viking, a division of Penguin Books USA Inc., 375 Hudson Street, New York, New York 10014, U.S.A. and Penguin Books Canada Ltd., 2801 John Street, Markham, Ontario, Canada L3R 1B4

Produced by the Department of Special Publications,
The Metropolitan Museum of Art
Series Editor: Mary Beth Brewer
Front Cover Design: Marleen Adlerblum
Design: Nai Y. Chang
Printing and Binding: A. Mondadori, Verona, Italy

Library of Congress Cataloging-in-Publication Data
Mühlberger, Richard. What makes a Bruegel a Bruegel? / Richard Mühlberger.
p. cm.
"The Metropolitan Museum of Art."
Summary: Explores such art topics as style, composition, color, and subject matter as they relate to twelve works by Bruegel.
ISBN 0-87099-668-1 (MMA) ISBN 0-670-85203-1 (Viking)
1. Bruegel, Pieter, ca. 1525–1569—Criticism and interpretation—Juvenile literature. 2. Painting, Flemish—Juvenile literature. 3. Genre painting—16th century—Flanders—Juvenile literature. [1. Bruegel, Pieter, ca. 1525–1569. 2. Painting, Flemish. 3. Art appreciation.] I. Metropolitan Museum of Art (New York, N.Y.) II. Title.
ND673.B73M78 1993 759.9493—dc20 93-7578 CIP AC
10 9 8 7 6 5 4 3 2 1

ILLUSTRATIONS

All works are by Pieter Bruegel the Elder.

Pages 1 and 2: *The Harvesters,* oil on wood, $46\frac{1}{2} \times 63\frac{1}{4}$ in., 1565, The Metropolitan Museum of Art, Rogers Fund, 1919, 19.164.

Page 6: *The Artist and the Connoisseur,* pen and bistre ink, $10 \times 8\frac{1}{2}$ in., The Albertina, Bildarchiv der Österreichischen Nationalbibliothek, Vienna.

Page 8: *Hunting Wild Rabbits,* etching, $8\frac{7}{16} \times 11\frac{1}{8}$ in., The Metropolitan Museum of Art, Harris Brisbane Dick Fund, 1925, 25.2.11.

Page 9: *Big Fish Eat Little Ones,* engraving, $9 \times 11\frac{5}{8}$ in., The Metropolitan Museum of Art, Harris Brisbane Dick Fund, 1928, 28.4(22).

Page 10: *The Fall of Icarus,* oil on canvas, $29 \times 44\frac{1}{8}$ in., Musées royaux des Beaux-Arts de Belgique, Brussels.

Page 14: *Children's Games,* oil on panel, $46\frac{1}{2} \times 63\frac{3}{8}$ in., 1560, Kunsthistorisches Museum, Vienna.

Page 18: *The Fall of the Rebel Angels,* oil on panel, $46 \times 63\frac{3}{4}$ in., 1562, Musées royaux des Beaux-Arts de Belgique, Brussels.

Page 21: *Two Monkeys,* oil on panel, $7\frac{7}{8} \times 9$ in., 1562, © Bildarchiv Preußischer Kulturbesitz, Berlin, 1993; photograph, Jörg P. Anders.

Page 22: *The Tower of Babel,* oil on panel, $44\frac{7}{8} \times 61$ in., 1563, Kunsthistorisches Museum, Vienna.

Page 26: *The Adoration of the Kings,* oil on panel, $43\frac{3}{4} \times 32\frac{3}{4}$ in., 1564, reproduced by courtesy of the Trustees, The National Gallery, London.

Page 28: *The Harvesters,* oil on wood, $46\frac{1}{2} \times 63\frac{1}{4}$ in., 1565, The Metropolitan Museum of Art, Rogers Fund, 1919, 19.164.

Pages 32–33: *Hunters in the Snow,* oil on panel, $46 \times 63\frac{3}{4}$ in., 1565, Kunsthistorisches Museum, Vienna.

Page 36: *The Land of Cockaigne,* oil on panel, $20\frac{1}{2} \times 30\frac{3}{4}$ in., 1567, Alte Pinakothek, Munich; photograph, Artothek, Munich.

Page 38: *The Wedding Banquet,* oil on panel, $44\frac{7}{8} \times 64\frac{1}{8}$ in., Kunsthistorisches Museum, Vienna.

Page 43: *The Peasant Dance,* oil on panel, $44\frac{7}{8} \times 64\frac{5}{8}$ in., Kunsthistorisches Museum, Vienna.

Pages 44–45: *The Parable of the Blind,* oil on canvas, $33\frac{7}{8} \times 60\frac{5}{8}$ in., 1568, Galleria Nazionale di Capodimonte, Naples; photograph, Erich Lessing/Art Resource, New York.

Page 47: *The Wedding Dance,* oil on panel, $46\frac{7}{8} \times 61\frac{1}{4}$ in., ca. 1566, © The Detroit Institute of Arts, City of Detroit Purchase.

Page 49: *The Census at Bethlehem,* oil on panel, $45\frac{5}{8} \times 64\frac{3}{4}$ in., 1566, Musées royaux des Beaux-Arts de Belgique, Brussels.

CONTENTS

The Artist and the Connoisseur

With ink and a fine-nib pen, Pieter Bruegel the Elder carefully portrayed an artist at work. Some say that this is a self-portrait, in which case it would be the only known likeness of Bruegel.

Meet Pieter Bruegel

The paintings of Pieter Bruegel the Elder take viewers back almost four hundred fifty years. The artist had a particular liking for peasants, the hardworking rural people who provided his country with food. It is said he dressed like them to go unnoticed to their weddings and fairs. Bruegel showed these joyous festivities in some of his most famous paintings, but other images by him suggest that famine, incurable diseases, and poverty constantly plagued the peasants. Yet they remained his favorite subject, and he painted them with honesty and compassion.

Bruegel's Point of View
Before you begin to read this book, flip through the pages to see Bruegel's vantage point. Quite often, he seems to have looked at a scene from up high to paint it; he liked this bird's-eye view for showing large groups of people. At other times, he preferred being down to earth. In either case, he was never really up or down, but was actually in his studio imagining the scene. His secret was to draw pictures of everything he saw around him. Then, when it came time to paint, he could piece together his composition from all of these references, knowing from them what things looked like from above or from straight on. Through his choices of vantage points, Bruegel made these experiences a gift to his viewers. It was one of the ways he made his paintings special; this book will explore many more.

In spite of the fact that Pieter Bruegel the Elder became the greatest artist of his age, the date of his birth is unknown. Even the year is debated, but scholars say that it was no earlier than 1520 and no later than 1530. The little-known artist credited with being his teacher is Pieter Coecke van Aelst. In 1551, the year after his teacher's death, Pieter Bruegel the Elder became a member of the Brotherhood, or Guild, of Saint Luke in Antwerp, Belgium, making him a full-fledged artist. From then on, only a few more facts about his life are certain.

Between 1551 and 1553, Bruegel traveled in France, Switzerland, and Italy, taking routes that were unknown to most tourists. His awe of the Alps was recorded in a remarkable series of drawings, and he later made landscape painting one of his specialties. During his trip, he also learned how to execute miniature paintings, very small pictures with every detail finely rendered. This skill was useful in filling up the crowded scenes that became one of his trademarks.

Hieronymous (Jerome) Cock, an enterprising publisher in Antwerp, hired Bruegel to supply his Print Shop of the Four Winds with drawings to be made into engravings. (An engraving is a type of print made on paper from an image cut into a metal plate.) For the decade after his trip, Bruegel produced one design after another, and engravings spread the artist's work far and wide. Even after 1563, when Bruegel moved from Antwerp to Brussels, his partnership with Cock continued. This is the period during which Bruegel also produced his finest paintings.

The reason for Bruegel's move was his marriage to Mayken Coecke, the daughter of his former teacher. She lived in Brussels with her widowed mother, Mayken Verhulst, an accomplished watercolor painter. By the time of his marriage, Bruegel was well known for his talents.

HUNTING WILD RABBITS

Bruegel combined a gently winding river, sailboats, church steeples, a windmill, and a prosperous port city to represent his homeland. The rugged cliff and wild terrain suggest the countryside he saw on a trip over the Alps to Italy.

He attracted commissions from the rich and powerful of Antwerp, Brussels, and other parts of the Low Countries, right to the end of his days. After Bruegel died prematurely in 1569, his mother-in-law helped his widow raise the couple's two sons. When they were old enough to study art, their grandmother was their first teacher.

More Than Meets the Eye

Today, the part of Europe where Bruegel lived is called Belgium, but in his lifetime the region was known as the Netherlands (meaning "low lands" or "low countries"), a name that now refers to Holland, the country north of Belgium. Bruegel's country was under the rule of Spain. Having a foreign king caused severe unrest, and so did the struggles of the new Protestant religions as they tried to gain a foothold in the Catholic Low Countries. Themes stemming from these conflicts are common in Bruegel's paintings, but they can be missed easily because the artist's imagery is deceptively simple.

Bruegel was the greatest artist of his lifetime in the Low Countries and one of the most celebrated artists of all time, but his works often pose riddles. Countless books and articles have been written about what his art means, and scholars continue to puzzle over it. Their opinions provide insight into Bruegel's paintings. Finding out what makes a Bruegel a Bruegel requires describing not just what is on the surface of his paintings, but what he hid under them as well.

GRANDIBVS EXIGVI SVNT PISCES PISCIBVS ESCA. Siet sone dit hebbe ick seer langhe ghehoorten dat die groote visschen de cleyne eten

BIG FISH EAT LITTLE ONES

In this print, one of Bruegel's many engravings, a fisherman says to his child, "Ecce," the Latin word for "behold." The caption under them continues, "See, son, I have long known that big fish eat little fish." This popular proverb was used to call attention to greedy landowners set on increasing their fortunes at the expense of the peasants who worked their land. This practice is one of a number of injustices Bruegel illustrated through the use of silly and seemingly innocent sayings.

The Fall of Icarus

Pieter Bruegel loved to paint sweeping landscapes and candid views of ordinary people. He also had a unique way of telling stories. In *The Fall of Icarus*, all are combined. The landscape and the figures are easy to study and appreciate, but the story is cleverly concealed. A thorough search of the painting is necessary to find Icarus and to discover what his fall from the skies meant to Bruegel and his contemporaries.

The ancient Greeks first told the story of Icarus, and it was known to Europeans of Bruegel's day through a famous book called

Metamorphoses, written by the Roman poet Ovid, who lived from 43 B.C. to about A.D. 17. He told how the mythical inventor Daedalus, the father of Icarus, found a way to fly by making wings of wax and feathers. Father and son donned their wings, and as they soared higher and higher, Daedalus warned Icarus not to get too near the sun. But it was too late. The sun melted the wax from the boy's wings, and, as the feathers fell, so did Icarus. Ovid wrote that Daedalus continued his journey, calling, "Icarus, where are you? Tell me where to find you!"

Blind Witnesses

In Bruegel's painting, Icarus is seen crashing into the sea, his legs disappearing in the water near the fancy ship in the lower right corner. Ovid stated that a plowman, a shepherd, and a fisherman were witnesses to the flight, and all are included here. Because the plowman is nearest the viewer and wears a bright red shirt, he is the most conspicuous. His eyes are on the earth, which he methodically prepares for the planting of crops. Every step he takes is careful so he is sure not to slip off the embankment. He certainly represents the opposite of Daedalus and Icarus.

On a shelf of land below the plowman, the shepherd looks up lazily, missing man's first flight. With his feet solidly planted on the earth, he, like the plowman, seems lost in his own world. The fisherman, in the lower right corner of the painting, is no help to Icarus, even though the

youth's body is close enough to his fishing lines to become entangled in them. Like the others, the fisherman is looking in the wrong direction.

None of the "witnesses" is aware of the poor boy's plight. To them and many others in Bruegel's day, the meaning of Icarus's fall was that ambition is futile. People saw Bruegel's painting as a warning to be content with one's lot. But others interpreted it as a lesson about the blindness of the plowman, the shepherd, and the fisherman, none of whom could see the value of Daedalus's new idea or Icarus's need for help.

11

A Magical View of the World

While the trio of peasants are blind to what goes on around them, Bruegel was not. Choosing a high vantage point, as though he himself were flying, the artist depicted the scene as if he were looking down on the three different levels of the embankment, skillfully painting his characters so that the story unfolds one section at a time. Then he looked out to create the beautiful landscape, a coastal panorama so vast that it seems to show continents beyond the pink and white cities. The galleons, closer by, might be ships of exploration set to circumnavigate the world. In fact, the first such voyage was completed at about the time of

Bruegel's birth. By putting these ships in his painting, Bruegel reminded his contemporaries that there were still people like Daedalus in the world.

Using a bird's-eye view, Bruegel depicted everything beneath him in minute detail. At the same time, however, he depicted other elements as if he could see far out to what seems like the edge of the world. In real life, it is impossible to look down and outward on a scene at the same time, but Bruegel's painting lets both happen at once. Because the artist knew how to combine these two viewpoints in one picture, his viewers receive a magical view of the world.

Children's Games

One of Bruegel's sixteenth-century countrymen wrote, "The world and all its activity is only a children's game." Uninhibited and honest, children do all the things that are natural for human beings, but they also imitate adults, exaggerating the good and the bad. For Bruegel, with his interest in human nature, they were a perfect subject. In his painting *Children's Games*, humanity is seen in miniature.

Bruegel painted an entire town inhabited by about two hundred fifty children. At first the image seems to capture a holiday, but soon it becomes clear that the painting is meant to be an encyclopedia of children's games. Because most of them are still played today, eighty-four have been identified, while others not known to the twentieth century have yet to be recognized.

Mankind at Play

Bruegel did not want to emphasize one game above the others. Not able to crowd them all up front, he painted them as if looking down at them from above so that none is blocked from view. While the distant children are smaller than the ones up front, their costumes are still bright. No matter where the children are, even in the shadows, Bruegel painted them as if they were in the noonday sun.

At first it looks as though the boys and girls are scattered at random, like jacks thrown on the ground. But Bruegel knew how to organize large crowds into patterns. The figures in the foreground of the painting are arranged in lines that fan out from the lower left corner and catch the viewer's eye first. Of course, being formed of children, the lines refuse to be exactly straight! The youngsters in the street behind them are placed in small groups that form a back-and-forth curving line.

Games easy to spot are leapfrog, blindman's buff, tumbling, walking with stilts, and playing with hoops. Many of the activities are improvised, such as hanging from the railing in front of the large yellow building or, across the street, riding the fence as if it were a pony. Others require simple equipment, like tops, which children can be seen spinning on the side porch of the yellow building, or dolls, with which others play inside the door of the brown building in the left foreground. As far as the eye can see, games can be found. Even the river on the left reveals swimmers.

Pretending to Be Big

In the center of the painting, a mock wedding takes place. With solemn faces, children accompany the girl-bride, who wears a crown. They walk slowly, guided by an older girl who seems to have played the game before. Near the entrance to the brown building is another procession in which children with covered heads follow the leader, who carries a blue blanket, pretending it is a baby on the way to its christening.

Bruegel made all of the children's faces similar. Differences in clothing are also slight, and not many colors are used. But each child looks like an individual because of the way the artist painted the bodies: No two are alike. After all, it is in the figures' movements that the viewer can tell what games are being played. By focusing not on personalities but on the games, Bruegel gave them a universal meaning.

The Fall of the Rebel Angels

Life was short for most people in the sixteenth century. Few adults outlived poverty, famine, and disease long enough to witness the infancy of their grandchildren. But even the most miserable person could take comfort in the angels. All those who believed deeply in God also believed in them. The Bible distinguished the good and faithful angels from the fallen angels, or demons.

The fall of the rebel angels was a traditional subject in art that warned people against pride, one of the seven deadly sins. Paintings that showed the differences between the beautiful, faithful angels and the weird, ugly monsters the rebellious angels became made viewers feel it was worthwhile to try to be humble.

Tumbling from a great globe of light that represents heaven, the good angels are confined to the top of the picture. Some sound their long, curved trumpets while others brandish swords and poke monsters with staffs. Each of these silver weapons has a cross at the top. The leader, Saint Michael the Archangel, is in the middle, appearing amazingly tall and slender in his shiny armor and full-length cloak. Instead of using his wings, he simply climbs across the pile of scoundrels beneath him, methodically slashing away at these incredible creatures. Floating to the left of Saint Michael is a glorious angel with golden hair and a billowing garment.

The monsters piled below are made of familiar shapes combined in bizarre ways. One is a musical instrument sporting lobster's claws.

Another appears as an artichoke sprouting butterfly's wings, warrior's arms, and a tail of bright red. Some, garbed in pieces of armor, answer the trumpet call of the faithful angels.

Haughty Spirits

While the handsome angel is typical of all the good angels, the agitated shrew at the bottom center of the painting is the embodiment of fallen pride. Her head is in profile against a gigantic cracked egg from which a bird-lobster is about to emerge. Elbows up, hands clenched in fists, this once beautiful angel is screaming at the top of her lungs.

In Bruegel's day, some found these creatures amusing, and they remain so today. The figures were meant to terrify sinners of doing wrong, and to inspire the pious to stay with the angels.

Two Monkeys

What an odd prison Bruegel created for his two red-headed monkeys! Chained to a ring bolt in a thick-walled lookout, the tropical creatures shiver in the cold, wet air of the Low Countries. They are also out of nuts, and hungry!

One exotic monkey probably served Bruegel as a model for both animals in this small painting. Monkeys were exceedingly rare in Europe and must have been carried from Africa by a sailor on one of the trade vessels that plied Antwerp's harbor. Most artists, upon seeing such a fascinating little beast, would sketch it for future reference, since monkeys were often shown in religious paintings as the Devil in disguise. Because of their uninhibited playfulness, monkeys also represented a variety of man's particularly nasty sins.

Bruegel's monkeys are certainly not enjoying themselves, nor are they part of a religious painting. In fact, this is one of the first paintings ever to show animals alone, by themselves. But it is not meant to be a nature study or a portrait of the animals; Bruegel used the monkeys in their prison to represent or symbolize something. Scholars who love and study Bruegel's art have presented many different ideas about what this painting might mean.

Because Spain ruled the Low Countries, many patriotic citizens of these territories felt they were in bondage. Some say that the monkeys represent the oppressed condition of Bruegel's countrymen, while others think the painting presents a moral point. The sins represented by the monkeys are what keep them shackled and deprived of the freedom seen through the opening of their cell. Even the nut-shells in the painting take on special significance, serving as symbols of the emptiness of worldly goods. No matter what the artist's specific intention was, one thing is certain: Bruegel was very proud of the painting, for he signed it and dated it with the Roman numerals MDLXII (meaning 1562), which appear as though carved in the stone.

Animals and Architecture

The artist took the color of the monkey's ruddy fur and used it throughout his painting. The animals' shapes are repeated in the architecture, too. The curve of the arch above them repeats curves in their bodies: their tails, the bend of the left foreleg of the monkey near the signature, and the outline of the second monkey's back. These rounded lines contrast with the sharp, straight edges of the ledge on which the furry prisoners sit. Skillfully using color and line, Bruegel unified the animals with the architecture.

The Tower of Babel

"Babel" describes the terrible din that occurs when everyone starts talking at once and no one can understand what anyone else is saying. The story of how this word came to stand for verbal confusion is recorded in Genesis, the first book of the Bible.

Originally, Babel was the Hebrew word for Babylon, the ancient city in Mesopotamia where, according to the Old Testament, Noah's ancestors settled after the flood. On the flat plains of what is now Iraq, they decided to build a tower that reached to heaven, but God knew the project was in vain. To put a stop to it, he gave all the builders and planners different languages "so that they may not understand one another's speech." The Bible states that until then, "the whole earth was of one language."

Topsy-Turvy Nonsense

Bruegel's fanciful tower is partly finished, partly unfinished, and partly already in ruins! Leaning dangerously backward and to the left, it is surrounded by an impressive town. At the base of the tower is a port where building supplies are delivered, and in the lower left corner is a busy stoneyard being inspected by Nimrod, the biblical king at the time the tower was built. He shows more interest in the homage being given him than in the exacting and strenuous work of the stonemasons. Everyone in the picture seems confident that this ambitious and crazy building scheme will succeed.

Only one ancient description of the Tower of Babel was known in Bruegel's day, that of the Greek historian Herodotus, who is called the Father of History. He wrote of a tower that was seven levels high, just as Bruegel showed it. He described square sections linked by stairs, but Bruegel made the sections round in his painting, connecting them by a spiral ramp all around the outside. For the shape and interior details of the tower, the artist's basic inspiration was the Colosseum, the most famous ancient ruin in Rome. Bruegel must have studied it carefully when he visited Rome ten years before painting this picture.

Bruegel's tower is nonsensical. With topsy-turvy abandon, he painted ramps and stairways that go nowhere or are obstructed. He invented an outer tower that, high up, has doorways and windows to nowhere, and an inner tower that

would have a spectacular view if its windows weren't blocked. Perhaps Bruegel meant to create a picture of confusion to reveal what the Tower of Babel signifies, as well as to show how silly people's ambitions can be. The confusing languages that were inflicted on the tower workers must also have interested Bruegel, for the Spanish rulers of the Low Countries could not even speak his tongue! Bruegel's painting *The Tower of Babel*, therefore, may be as much a comment on the contemporary scene as an illustration of a biblical story.

Details True to Bruegel's Time
Many of Bruegel's larger paintings (this one is five feet wide) are filled with numerous tiny details that can be explored endlessly. The sprawling town is of Bruegel's own time, as are the sixteenth-century vessels delivering supplies to the port. The construction equipment is contemporary as well.

Scrutinizing all the figures and machines in this painting provides a lesson in the engineering and building techniques of 1563. Some of the most interesting details are lifts and pulleys that transfer large stones from the port to the middle level of the tower, where the structure seems to merge with a mountain. Yet although the figures, houses, and machines in Bruegel's painting were of his time, nothing remotely like the tower itself existed in the Low Countries or anywhere else in Europe.

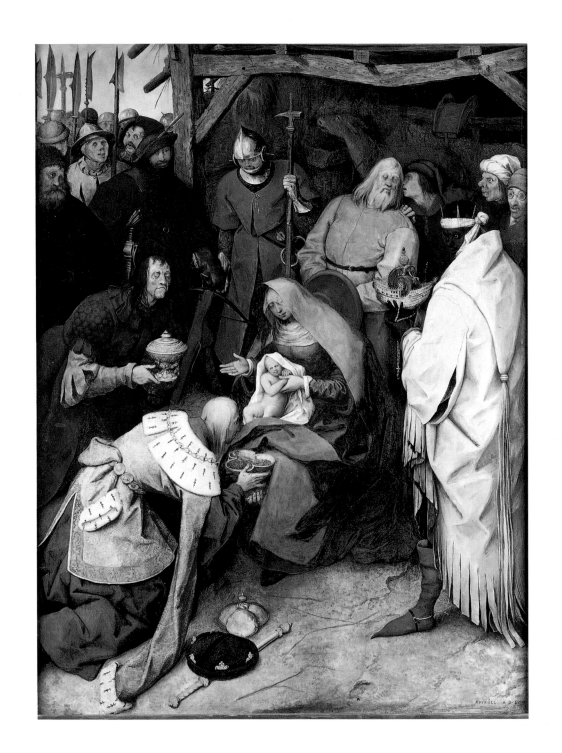

The Adoration of the Kings

When Bruegel painted Bible scenes, he looked closely at the people around him and included them. In his painting *The Adoration of the Kings*, the kings, or wise men, wear strange, imaginative garments, but their faces must have seemed ordinary to sixteenth-century eyes. So did everyone else in the painting. One of the reasons Bruegel filled this traditional scene with familiar faces is that he wanted his viewers to enter the event with their hearts and feel at home there. To make the painting easy to enter, Bruegel left an opening in the front. The place between the two kings in the foreground is where devout viewers can imagine they are standing or kneeling.

Bruegel followed the familiar story from the New Testament that says that when the wise men found Jesus, they "fell down and worshiped" him. Other details are true to popular traditions— there were three kings, one of them from North Africa, and a donkey to warm Jesus with his breath. (Bruegel showed the donkey almost lost in the monochromatic interior of the shed.)

Why the Soldiers?
Two of Bruegel's kings are so old that they find it difficult and painful to bend or kneel. The one in front, wearing a rich, white fur of ermine, has caught the interest of Jesus with his handsome gift of incense in a gold bowl. So splendid is the vessel that the soldier who stands and watches from under the rustic shed is wide-eyed. The second wise man holds another gold bowl, and the third, standing to the right, carries the most incredible gift of all. It is a boat made of precious metals, a rare nautilus shell, and rich, colorful jewels.

Joseph, Mary's husband, stands behind her, listening to the whispered words of a young man. If Mary and the two older kings stood up, they would be about the height of the African king, the tallest figure in the painting. Giving the four figures extra height was one of Bruegel's ways to show their importance.

Soldiers and weapons might seem out of place in a sacred scene, but armed men, spears, and a crossbow appear in the painting. Soldiers were hated in the Low Countries in Bruegel's day because they served a foreign king. Are Bruegel's soldiers changing allegiance from their worldly ruler to a spiritual one, the holy child? Or are they merely a military escort for the three kings? Perhaps their presence is meant to remind viewers that Jesus was surrounded by soldiers during his last days on earth, just as they surround him here.

The Harvesters

After Bruegel moved from the noisy, prosperous city of Antwerp to Brussels, a more elegant place where his wife wanted to live, he kept in touch with a number of his friends from Antwerp. One of them was a man of great wealth named Niclaes Jonghelinck. He appreciated Bruegel's talent, and was the first to collect his works, eventually owning sixteen paintings. In 1565, Jonghelinck commissioned Bruegel to create a series of paintings on the subject of the months of the year to decorate the walls of a reception room in his new mansion in Antwerp. Five of the paintings still exist today, including *The Harvesters* and *Hunters in the Snow*. Most scholars believe that each painting represents a time of the year, or a two-month span, meaning that one painting is lost. Others insist that there was a painting for every month of the year, in which case a treasure of seven is missing!

"Grain Month" Is August

It was not a new idea to illustrate the seasons or the months of the year, but Bruegel's paintings were the first to glorify the landscape. He painted the countryside because of its own beauty and interest, as well as to show how much human beings shape it and are shaped by it. Because the harvest is in summertime, it seems logical that *The Harvesters* represents July and August. In fact, August was known as *Koornemaand* (*koorn* meaning "grain" and *maand* meaning "month") in the Low Countries in Bruegel's day.

The people Bruegel showed harvesting the wheat probably also tilled the soil and planted the seeds. Cutting and bundling wheat is hard work, so the laborers take turns lunching or napping. The contrasts between strenuous labor, rest, and exhaustion can be seen in their postures. Bruegel gave them round faces that do not reveal as much as their bending, sagging, twisting, and sprawling bodies do.

A Lazy Lunch Breaks a Hard Day

By depicting the scene as if viewing it from high above, Bruegel allowed an unusual look at the peasants' lunch break. To improvise seating, the figures have moved hay bundles near the tree that shades them from the sun. Bruegel grouped together the hay, the sleeping man, and the peasants enjoying lunch, making them seem connected to the tree trunk.

In contrast to the lunch crowd, the workers are placed against the dense growth of golden wheat. Like sculptors they chisel away, reducing the field to even piles that appear smaller and smaller as they extend to the bushy verge of the farm. Beyond the farm, the hamlet where the peasants live snuggles in between hills, a small church poking its steeple above the houses. In the left background, wheat is being carted away, perhaps to the port in the distance. Scholars say the port may be based on drawings of Lake Geneva that Bruegel possibly made during his earlier travels through Switzerland.

Showing Less to Say More
Bruegel is as famous for what he does not show in a painting as for what he does show. In the foreground, the cut piles and stacks of wheat are painted rich yellow, with brown lines to indicate individual shafts. But when the artist pictured the field, he used his brown paint sparingly along the upright edge of the wheat. In fact, for the top of the wheat field, he abandoned brown entirely, describing this area simply as one solid expanse of yellow paint. There, Bruegel did not need to indicate the top of every shaft, because from the foreground, the viewer already knows that the field is made up of many individual stalks. In this way, Bruegel says much by showing little.

Hunters in the Snow

Using only a few colors, Bruegel painted a winter scene that is familiar to anyone who has trudged through snow. The tracks of the three hunters, their dogs, and a rabbit that has disappeared out of sight are all that mar the pristine surface of recently fallen snow. The hunters are probably near home, for the one in the lead seems to know a shortcut down the steep slope to the houses below. Four trees mark the way. Bruegel placed them so that they cut across the edge of the drop. If the two trees in the foreground were connected at their bases, they would form a line that goes far beyond the hunters all the way to the jagged peaks of the mountains in the upper right corner.

Tired Men and Beasts

The steep, snowy slope separates the hunters from the village. It is not known how long the three have been away from home hunting food for their families and neighbors, but the gap between them and their village suggests they have been gone for a long time. With their return, they bring their bounty. The game bag of the nearest hunter is almost full, and the second hunter carries a small animal over his shoulder. As they tread silently down the slope, they lower their heads. Like their pack of canine helpers, the hunters are tired. The tall, erect tree trunks stand in stark contrast to the men's bent bodies. The

33

trees, placed so they march from the foreground toward the middle of the painting, and the steady pace of the hunters suggest a stalwart move forward in spite of the obstacles of cold and snow.

Faces That Do Not Show

The painting shows the hunters' tough determination in the face of the deadening weather of winter. It also is an engaging view of a village under snow. While the family on the left feeds a fire to prepare dinner for the guests at their inn, a gust of wind dislodges the inn sign, which, dangling from one hook, dumps the snow that

has collected on top of it into an eddy of cold air. The resulting puff of white powder and the slant of the cooking fire are the only hints that there is a wind. Some of the villagers below go about their daily business, but most seem to be playing hockey and making other sport on the frozen river. (In some paintings of Bruegel's day, ice skating represented the uncertainty of existence, for thin ice can break through at any minute. Here, though, there appears to be no danger.) Few seem to have prepared their houses for a freeze; smoke rises only from the chimneys beyond the skating pond.

Although the architecture in the painting is that of the Low Countries, the craggy mountains are Swiss in appearance, and the dogs and the hunters are universal, belonging to all places where the earth is white from November through February. Bruegel revealed none of the hunters' faces, yet oddly, that makes it easier to identify with them. Individual faces would be a point of difference with most viewers, for few faces are alike. But the bend of the hunters' legs against the drifts of snow makes it easy to imagine what being in their boots would be like.

Hunters in the Snow is one of the paintings Jonghelinck ordered, and scholars think it represents either November and December or January and February. It is a rare work for Bruegel, for few experts believe that the scene contains hidden meaning. Because this painting was so popular, it led many artists of the next century to specialize in winter landscapes.

The Land of Cockaigne

The Land of Cockaigne is a never-never land of luxury, easy living, and lots of food. Some believe that *Cockaigne* comes from a German word for a small sugar cake, but the origins of the imaginary place are not exactly known. In Dutch, which Bruegel spoke, such a place would be called *Luilekkerland, lui* meaning "lazy" and *lekker*

meaning "delicious." Bruegel brought a corner of Cockaigne to life in his unusual painting, taking many of his ideas about the legendary place from a description published two decades earlier. In that description, the writer did not praise Cockaigne; instead, he condemned the gluttony and sloth that prospered there.

In the painting, four men lie dazed from eating too much, but they are so addicted to the peculiar goodies around them that they long for more. Bruegel gave the men particular occupations to make them believable, for the painting is meant to say, "If this could happen to them, this could happen to you, too." On the left is a soldier, peering out from his strange shelter; nearby, a knight sprawls on top of his jousting lance. A bloated farmer, with his back to the viewer, has collapsed across his thresher. The fourth man is a well-to-do clerk, his legs spread like the dials of a clock over his fur-lined coat.

Loafers and Gluttons

The soldier's roof is tiled with cakes and pies. This will be dessert after the back fence, which is woven of linked sausages, is devoured. The lake is white because it is filled not with water, but with milk, meant to be served with the mountain of porridge that spills into it from the upper right corner of the picture. The man emerging from this mass has eaten his way from the other side! Constructed around the tree, a lopsided table holds even more food, and pancakes tumble from nowhere on the right side of the picture. Other examples of Bruegel's riotous imagination are a ready-to-eat ham and a broken egg with a knife in it, strutting

on chick's legs. By way of preparing a little picnic for anyone who might still be hungry, a cooked goose puts herself onto a platter set on a white cloth.

Bruegel designed this scene as though he saw it from a perch on a limb of the tree in the center of the painting. Because of this vantage point, the viewer is allowed to look straight down at the three men on the ground. It is easy to see that the round tree table is off kilter, as is the edge of the earth. The angles of their slant set the entire composition into a spin. Viewers who look at the middle of the painting too long might experience dizziness—probably what the men in the scene feel as they recover from their feasting!

No sooner had Bruegel completed *The Land of Cockaigne* than printed reproductions of the painting were made in the form of engravings, so that many people could own copies of the fanciful image. To make sure the picture taught the lesson that was intended, these lines were inscribed under it:

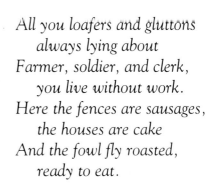

All you loafers and gluttons
   always lying about
Farmer, soldier, and clerk,
   you live without work.
Here the fences are sausages,
   the houses are cake
And the fowl fly roasted,
   ready to eat.

The Wedding Banquet

Wine and food take pride of place in this banquet scene. Villagers longed for weddings at least partly because extra victuals and special treats were dispensed. In fact, nuptial festivities became so crowded and rowdy that an imperial decree limited the number of guests. In Bruegel's painting, the invited sit at the long table while many others, hoping the law will be forgotten, crowd through the open door at the far left waiting for a chance to taste the wine and pudding being served in the foreground. The uninvited cannot be kept out of the thrashing barn-turned-banquet hall, because the door is missing: Doubling as a tray, it is being heaved by the two serving men.

Bruegel painted the walls of the barn the same color as the wheat that usually filled it. Against this golden yellow, the various colors of the guests' costumes stand out. Red jackets and caps and white headdresses cause the eye to dart up and down the diagonal arrangement of people and inspect every one of them. At a wedding, the bride and groom should be the most important figures at the banquet, but here, surprisingly, they are harder to find than the two waiters.

Where Did the Groom Go?
The bride sits against a dark green blanket suspended from the wall. On her head is a narrow crown; a second crown hangs above her. To her left sit her parents. The bride's father is the only guest seated in an armchair, a place of honor. The monk at the end of the table, who probably

assisted in the church ceremony, talks to a mystery man. Scholars remain puzzled as to why this one guest, dressed as he is in a fine black doublet and obviously a member of the upper classes, is mixing with peasants at a simple wedding party.

In Bruegel's time, the groom would also wear a crown very like the bride's at his wedding, but none of the males in this picture sports one.

Some say the greedy fellow to the left of the bride, with his spoon lost in his mouth, is the groom, and those who elect him propose that the man at his side, apparently giving last-minute advice, is his father. Sitting immediately behind the serving man in the long white apron is a second candidate for groom, the fellow who leans back on his stool with mug raised, calling for a refill. A more attractive suggestion is that the groom is the well-dressed man pouring wine in the left corner of the painting; it would be appropriate for the groom to supply wine for the wedding guests and to serve personally at least

one round of it. A final, comical idea is that the groom is attached to the extra foot under the barn-door serving tray!

Two Lessons for All

Two bagpipers provide raucous melody for the guests' enjoyment. The one in the red jacket prepares his lips for playing another round of tunes as he fills his wide-open eyes with the sights of food and drink. Licking the bowl clean, the greedy child in the lower left is also interested in food. The emphasis on serving, eating, and drinking has led some to say that *The Wedding*

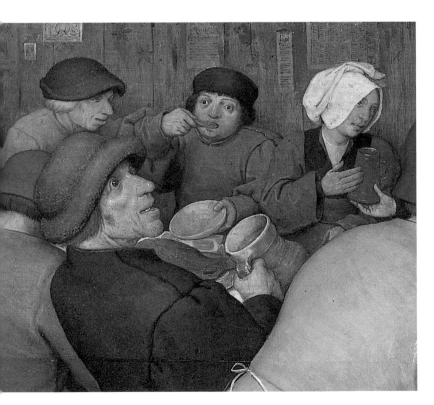

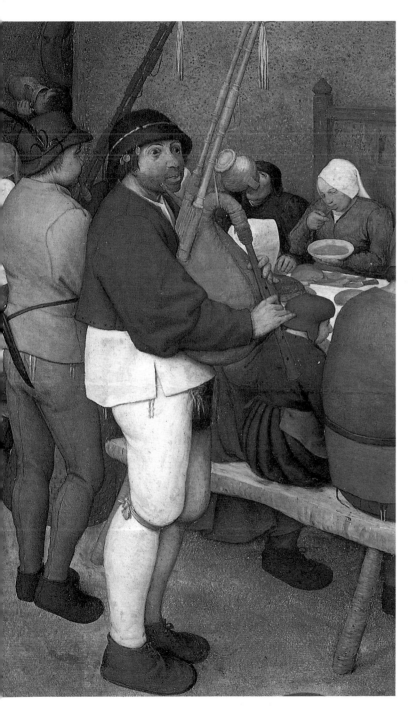

Banquet was meant as a warning against gluttony. If it is, a second reminder is also present in the painting.

The two sheaves of wheat that hang from a hook on the wall above the monk and the father of the bride represent the small share of crops all charitable farmers were expected to leave in the fields for the poor, the fatherless, and widows. Unable to find food elsewhere, these unfortunate people followed the farmers, collecting what was missed. Bruegel's lessons to eat and drink in moderation, and to share with the needy, are lessons for all people at all times.

The Peasant Dance

There is an old adage that says people never change, a point Bruegel proves in *The Peasant Dance*. So real are the feelings and emotions of the people he portrays that with a few changes of costume and architecture, the figures could be at a dance in any town in any country in the world today. Their outdoor party in the painting is a celebration, or *kermess*, in honor of a saint's birthday. Although the merrymakers ignore the church in the background and the image of the Virgin and Child attached to the tree on the right, they must be deeply grateful for the opportunity to put work aside and have fun.

The Youth Hears Only One Sound

Bruegel did not explain his paintings. In addition to being beautiful to look at, many have symbolic significance. In some, Bruegel's characters have such strong expressions or postures that the viewer must decide what is going on. An example of this is the pair of dancers in the foreground of *The Peasant Dance*. The older man with a spoon in his hat and the woman with the dress lined in yellow skip out from the right corner of the painting to join the other couples in an energetic dance. The woman can barely keep up with her partner's step, and she glances apprehensively at the other dancers. The man, perhaps inviting them to dance, too, yells to the kissing couple

at the far left—a woman who wears a white head covering and a man sporting a red hat. The men sitting around the table jokingly mime the young couple by reaching out to one another.

In the middle of this exchange is a bagpiper, his face puffed just like the bag between his arms. He seems unaware of the admiring young man at his elbow, who, in rapt attention, is learning how to play the difficult instrument. The mug the young man rests on his knee is a sociable one, meant to be passed around the table, but for the moment it is forgotten. On the other side of the piper, a girl teaches a younger child how to dance. They both are miniature adults in their proportions and costumes.

Hidden and Not So Hidden Sins

Bruegel's good-natured brush targeted a number of sins in the painting. By revealing them, he hoped to warn people away from them. One of the sins is drunkenness, illustrated by the behavior of the fellows at the table. A second set of sins is suggested in the peacock's feather trailing from the stylishly cocked hat of the young man with the piper. Peacock feathers often symbolized vanity and boastfulness. Other clues to sins the painting warns against are the kissing couple, and the man and woman at the gate of the big house with the red banner. Either the man is pulling the woman out to join in the dance, or the woman is trying to drag the man inside so they can do their kissing in private. Kissing was associated with marriage, and was considered improper behavior between strangers, a display of lustfulness. Lust was listed as one of the seven deadly sins. While morality lessons are often present in Bruegel's paintings, it is easy to forget them and become lost in his characters and the fun they are having. By abandoning his favored position from up high, Bruegel emphasized the fact that the viewer might be one of them, for good or for bad.

The Parable of the Blind

Bruegel's painting *The Parable of the Blind* was inspired by words Jesus spoke to his disciples. Instructing them not to pay any attention to those who criticized them, Jesus explained, "They be blind leaders of the blind. And if the blind lead the blind, both shall fall into the ditch" (Matt. 15:14).

Bruegel eliminated vivid color from his palette because he wanted to create a world like that of blindness. Everything is gray, blue, and brown. The leader of the group, a musician, tumbles backward into the swamp, his instrument at his side. The second man spills onto the lap of the first. The third man, with begging bowl and rosary cinched to his belt and shin guards on his legs, is jerked closer to these two. In an instant, the tug on the stick that links them together will be passed on to the next three men, and they will also go over the brink.

Their Fall Cannot Be Prevented

To emphasize that the march of the blind men is fated to disaster, Bruegel arranged the figures on a diagonal path from the upper left to the lower right of the painting. The steep roofs of the

pictures of them, so he had real models in his mind's eye when he painted this picture.

Blind Hearts and Souls

Bruegel was able to transform what he saw in everyday life into a meaningful allegory. The blind men in the painting are a clear warning: Do not put blind trust in blind leaders.

When the Bible speaks of blindness, it often refers not just to eyes that are closed to sight, but to a closed heart and soul as well. The result is spiritual blindness that robs a person of salvation and eternal life. This was considered a much more serious condition than blindness of the eyes. Bruegel certainly was thinking of such an affliction of the soul when he included the solidly built church with its tall stone steeple in the background of his painting. It represents a kind of spiritual hospital for those who are blind to faith, hope, and charity. Identified as an actual church that still stands in the village of Pede Sainte Anne, near Brussels, it was meant to convince Bruegel's viewers that the catastrophe of the blind men was real, too.

The Praise Continues

In the year that Bruegel painted *The Parable of the Blind,* he died. The date was September 9, 1569. His sons grew up to be painters, copying their father's works, and they trained their own sons to be painters as well. The family tradition lived on until the eighteenth century. Generation after generation of Brueghels (they replaced the *h* in

houses at the rear of their parade emphasize the men's downward journey. The artist also invented a precipice on one side of their path with the earth sloped toward it. The feet of the men who have not yet fallen struggle against sliding sideways as they shuffle forward.

Bruegel had many opportunities to observe blind men; unfortunately, they were a common sight in the cities. From time to time, he drew their name, which Pieter the Elder had removed) loved and respected the work of their founder. The dynasty produced many wonderful paintings, but no member of the family ever reached the greatness of Pieter Bruegel the Elder.

One of Bruegel's closest friends was the great geographer and map publisher Abraham Ortelius. When Bruegel died, Ortelius wrote that he was "the most perfect painter of the century." He then showed how deeply he admired Bruegel's art with these words: "But whether his being snatched away from us in the flower of his age was due to Death's mistake in thinking him older than he was on account of his extraordinary skill in art or rather to Nature's fear that his genius for imitation would bring her into contempt, I cannot say."

Ortelius was not the last to praise Bruegel's art extravagantly. Comical, heroic, meditative, spiritual, truthful—these are just a few of the adjectives used by generations of art lovers to express the magic of Bruegel's art.

THE WEDDING DANCE

Bruegel gave the viewer a bird's-eye view of this merry gathering, in which dancers and revelers move in a serpentine rhythm. The bride is seated before the "cloth of honor" at the top of the picture. The groom appears to be lost in the crowd, just as viewers are when they study the painting's details. Experiencing the picture this way makes Bruegel's world as lively now as it was for the wedding guests four and a half centuries ago.

What Makes a Bruegel

Bruegel was one of the first painters to celebrate the landscape, and he often pictured it from a bird's-eye view. He set religious and historical scenes in his own time and place.

1.

3.

2.

1. Bruegel loved to show the everyday pastimes of the peasants.

2. His subjects' characters are revealed through their poses rather than through their expressions.

3. Bruegel liked to simplify. Here, the faces in the crowd look very much the same.

4. Bruegel filled his paintings with detail.

4.